Basic Business

&

Commercial Law for Startups and Entrepreneurs

A Beginner's Guide

By

Chukwuemeka Mbah

BL, LLB, LLM-European and International Business Law

Copyright © 2018 by Chukwuemeka Christopher Mbah

All rights reserved.

No portion of this book may be reproduced in any form without written permission from the publisher or author, except as permitted by Nigerian copyright law.

This publication is designed to provide accurate and authoritative information in regard to the subject matter covered. It is sold with the understanding that neither the author nor the publisher is engaged in rendering legal, investment, accounting, or other professional services. While the publisher and author have used their best efforts in preparing this book, they make no representations or warranties with respect to the accuracy or completeness of the contents of this book and specifically disclaim any implied warranties of merchantability or fitness for a particular purpose. No warranty may be created or extended by sales representatives or written sales materials. The advice and strategies contained herein may not be suitable for your situation. You should consult with a professional when appropriate. Neither the publisher nor the author shall be liable for any loss of profit or any other commercial damages, including but not limited to special, incidental, consequential, personal, or other damages.

Quiver Publishers
09071007327

DEDICATION

This work is dedicated to my heavenly and earthly father, both fatherhood have inspired my concern for mother earth. Glory and thanks to them respectively.

ACKNOWLEDGEMENTS

I thank my heavenly father for the grace he availed me to deliver on this book. I would like to express my gratitude to my earthly father for putting me in this path. Also, to my supervisor Professor Tamas Fezer for his guidance and support every step of the way. His unique style of supervision and leadership contributed to the quality of this work. I am grateful to my family, friends and colleagues for their kind support. Worthy of mention are Mr. Jemba Moh, my mentor, Mrs. Miriam Kachikwu and the entire legal team at Seplat for upholding excellent corporate governance values with total compliance and adherence to regulatory requirements and industry best practices globally. To Goodness Armstrong, Obinna Edeh and Judith Ozoani, I say a big thank you for sacrificing your time to ensure this work comes out error free.

Table of Content

Introduction 6

Chapter 1.
Entity formation 9

Chapter 2.
Contracts 18

Chapter 3.
Risks & Due Diligence 31

Chapter 4.
Dispute Resolution 41

Chapter 5.
Labour & Employment 47

Chapter 6.
Business Ethics & Corporate Governance 55

Chapter 7.
Company Secretarial Services 59

Chapter 8.
Intellectual Property 63

Chapter 9.
5G of Retainer Arrangement 66

Chapter 10.
Future of Business Law 72

Conclusion 74

Introduction

When it comes to business and law, early distinction should be made between the *business of law* and the *law of business*. While the former concentrates on how lawyers commercialize their legal services the latter which happens to be our focus examines the formulation, interpretation and application of law to business.

To be an effective and efficient manager or to run a responsible and responsive organization in the post COVID-19 complex business environment, one must have an understanding of how the law impacts the bottom line. Yes, you can play by the rules, comply with local regulatory enactments, conform to international best practices, maintain high ethical standards, and still remain profitable.

No matter how your company playbook is wired, this book addresses legal areas in which everyone in business should have a level of familiarity in order to mitigate risks and reduce costs. The basics of contract law, corporate governance, dispute resolution, competition law and other allied concepts are covered. We will extend our intellectual voyage to further examine foreign and local case studies alongside current trends in business law. The intent of this module includes but not limited to ensuring that each participant understands the impact of these areas of the law on business decisions, and to be aware of, as well as manage risks associated with the legal aspects of daily business dealings.

I do not pretend to have an exhaustive module on Business and Commercial law here, as there is a plethora of topics on the subject beyond what can be compressed into this book. However, what was hand-picked to be in this book is designed and tailored to start you up or keep you going.

What is in it for you?

- Learn how to do some things yourself (yes you can, sometimes… must be careful)

- Learn how to negotiate a fair deal

- Learn how to keep yourself protected

- Learn the key things to look for when reviewing a legal document

- Learn what to look for when hiring an attorney

- Know what questions to ask when you do hire an attorney

Who is this for?

- Business owners

- Startup entrepreneurs

- Lawyers looking to brush up on business law.

- Anyone who can read and write.

CHAPTER 1

Entity Formation

Forming a business entity is an important way to protect oneself from liability, maximize profit, attract a caliber of clients and investors, etc. A business entity such as a corporation or limited liability company is legally a separate "person" from its owners. As an artificial person, it also has rights and obligations conferred on it by various legislative enactments. There are some key things to keep in mind when you go about *setting up* a business.

Filing Formation Paperwork

To *set up* most business entities, you must file a form with the state agency that handles business filings (this process varies depending on *the* country) along with a filing fee and other supporting documents. After the state receives and successfully processes your formation paperwork, you may receive a certificate confirming that your new company officially exists.

In North America for instance, one of the major supporting document(s) used is a corporate charter which is the equivalent of *memorandum and articles of association* used in some parts of Africa. A corporate charter, also known as a "charter" or "articles of incorporation," is a written document filed with the Secretary of State (or registrar in Canada) by the founders of a corporation. It details the major components of a company, such as its objectives, structure, and planned operations. If approved by the state, the company becomes a legal corporation. We will proceed to examine steps in forming a legal entity, using Nigeria as a case study.

In Nigeria, a company can either be a private or public company which is further sub divided depending on the liability of its members as regards its shares. A company can be limited by shares, limited by guarantee or unlimited. To concretize a business idea into a company in Nigeria, you can choose from among the following legal entities.

1. **Sole Trader/Proprietor**

    A *Sole Trader* is a business enterprise run by a single person. It is the simplest form of business entity, not mandatorily requiring a company registration. In such a company, the sole trader is personally responsible for all aspects of the business and has unlimited liability to all debts and obligations. There is no difference between the owner and the trade as the law sees them as one. In official documents, it is usually captured as the owner (e.g- John Bosky) trading under the name and style of his business (e.g. John Bosky Enterprises). When it is more than one proprietor running this kind of venture, it becomes a partnership (e.g. - John Bosky & Sons). Both Sole Proprietorship and Partnerships are registered as Business Names under Part B of CAMA- Section 588(1).

2. **Private Limited Liability Company**

    Often designated as "LTD," Private Limited Liability Company is an entity separate from its shareholders, who enjoy limited liability. This means that their personal possessions remain separate, and their risk is reduced to only the money they have invested in the company in form of shares. The major requirements for incorporating a private limited company in Nigeria include but not limited to:

- The total number of members usually doesn't exceed 50. Members here typically refer to shareholders and this excludes the employees of the company.
- The company must have a registered office in Nigeria.
- A minimum of 2 people above 18 years of age must subscribe to the Memorandum & Articles of Association.
- The name of the company must not be misleading, prohibited, or restricted under the *Companies and Allied Matters Act* (CAMA) as regulated by the Corporate Affairs Commission (CAC).

3. **Public Limited Liability Company**

    Often designated as "PLC" a Public Limited Liability Company unlike a private limited one, is allowed to be publicly listed and sell its shares to the public. This is often done under the platform of the Nigerian Stock Exchange (NSE) and regulated by the Securities and Exchange Commission (SEC). The minimum share capital and cost of running a public limited company is considerably higher than that of a private limited liability company. Therefore, a public limited company is better suited for large organizations.

4. **Company Limited by Guarantee**

    Often designated as "LTD/GTE," a Company Limited by guarantee in Nigeria is an alternative type of corporation used primarily for non-profit organizations that require legal personality. A company limited by guarantee does not usually have a share capital or shareholders, but instead has members who act as guarantors. The guarantors give an undertaking to contribute a nominal amount (typically very small) in the event of the winding up of the company.

5. *Unlimited Liability Company*

Often designated as "ULTD" or "UnLTD," an Unlimited Liability company is a type of company having the liability of its members unlimited by the memorandum to any amount. In the event of being wound up, and its liabilities exceed its assets (in other words, where it is insolvent), the liquidator will go to the members asking for contribution (i.e. in proportion to the numbers of shares they hold) to make good the deficit. The joint, several, and non-limited liability of the members to meet any insufficiency in the assets of the company (to settle its outstanding liabilities if any exist) applies only upon the formal liquidation of the company.

6. ***Incorporated Trustees***

Incorporated Trustees are non-business and non-profit making organizations formed to facilitate the acquisition of corporate personality by a community of persons bound together by a common interest which may include but not limited to custom, religion, nationality, OR any association of person**s** established for religious, educational, literary, scientific, social developments, sporting or charitable purpose: section 590 of CAMA. It can be registered under Part C of CAMA and can however, operate without registration but cannot take advantage of the corporate identity of the trustees.

Benefits of entity formation in Nigeria

The following are a few of the benefits:

a) You can protect your personal assets and determine your extent of liability

b) May minimize your tax exposure and attract some

Government incentives (consult your tax lawyer for advice)

c) It enhances your business credibility, creates brand awareness and legitimacy

d) Creates easy access to credit facility from Banks and Investors

e) Gives easy access to grants from Government, Development partners, and iNGOs

f) It makes you look serious and attracts more customers/clients

g) There is little or no limitation to expressing your creativity or ability to innovate

h) A lot of leadership and management decisions are within your control

i) Gives you anonymity

Advice & Tips:

Individual/Proprietors can register *business names* without the services of a legal practitioner, Chartered Accountant or Chartered Secretary.

CHAPTER 2

Contracts

What is a Contract?

A valid contract is a legally binding agreement that recognizes and regulates the rights and duties of the parties to the agreement. A contract becomes legally enforceable when it meets the requirements and approval of the law.

Basically, a contract is a promise for a promise (or an act). A contract (express or implied) has 4 elements:

1. Capacity (your ability to enter into a contract);
2. Mutual agreement ("meeting of the minds" or "*Consensus Ad Idem*") as to clear offer and acceptance without counter-offers;

3. Furnished Consideration (something of value exchange);
4. Legality (only legal deals - no slavery, usury, drug deals, etc).

A Contract becomes invalid and unenforceable if it is missing one or more of the above requirements.

Consideration – is the bedrock of a contract: it is the *"this-for-that"* concept - it can be an action or refrain from taking action. However, illusory promises, gifts, past considerations, already obligated to do and moral obligations cannot be considered as valid forms of consideration.

Boilerplate

Boilerplate clauses, also known as standard, miscellaneous, or general clauses, are clauses that are found at the end of most legal documents. These provisions address a range of things such as what happens if a document is declared unenforceable, how disputes will be resolved, which laws govern the contract, and more.

General clauses may be considered secondary to the significant parts of the document because they use standardized language and are buried near the end of the agreement. However, they should not be mistaken as unimportant, and parties should pay as much attention to them as they do to the main clauses such as payment.

Below are some of the questions Boilerplate clauses seek to raise

Clauses	Questions/Standards
Costs	Losing party bears the cost of suits
Alternative Dispute Resolution (ADR)	How do you intend to resolve disputes? Mediation? Arbitration? Both?
Governing Law	What state's law will apply in a dispute?
Jurisdiction	Where a lawsuit must be filed in a dispute
Waiver	Agreeing to give up the right to sue for a breach of a part of a particular provision without giving up future claims regarding that provision. (i.e *just because I don't enforce it now, doesn't mean I won't enforce it later*)
Severability	invalid provisions, will not invalidate the whole

	agreement
Integration	This is a clause in a written contract which declares that contract to be the complete and final agreement between the parties. It is often placed at or towards the end of the contract. Any pre-contractual material which the parties wish to be incorporated into the contract needs to be assembled with it or explicitly referred to in the contractual documentation. Otherwise, it stands invalidated by the integration clause.

Notice	What constitutes proper notice and when is it deemed to have been received?
Relationships	Defining clearly what the relationship is and what it is not: you are not a

	partnership/no employment or agency relationship created.
Assignability/delegation	Can you assign the rights/delegate the duties under the contract?
Warranties	Promises and assurances regarding the contract obligations (i.e. I warrant that I own this stuff I am selling to you in good shape)
Indemnity	One party covenants to compensate for the loss incurred to the other party due to the acts of the Indemnitor or any other party.
Counterparts	To sign a contract in counterparts means that each party to the

	contract will be signing different, but identical, copies of the contract. All of the different copies, together will complete a single agreement and any of these copies can be treated as an original for evidentiary purposes.

Remedies:

Remedies could come in different forms when there is a breach. These include:

Compensatory - to compensate you for the breach: put you where you would have been if no breach occurred.

Consequential - have the breaching side pay for all the problems that arose from the breach (usually limited)

Punitive - only available if the breaching party was willful and reckless, usually never awarded - only by statute or a business tort claim - contract law isn't much about punishment

Question: Are oral contracts valid?

Answer: **Yes**. Express contracts are stated in words, whether oral or written. Problem is evidence ("he said, she said"). Some deals must be evidenced in writing: paying another's debt; sale of land interest (property law); performance takes longer than 1 year , and sale of goods ($500 and above for some jurisdictions).

Question: Can an email be a contract?

Answer: **Yes**. A contract is a promise for a promise/act. If a series of written documents evidences(**evidence)** all the requirements of a contract - you have a contract! This raises the point of implied contracts: implied by conduct/actions (versus words), implied by law court will create a contract to avoid one side benefitting at the expense of the other.

Question: Is silence acceptance?

Answer: **No**. The *Offeror* cannot impose a duty to the *Offeree* to do something, as there is no previous obligation, **BUT:**

There are few exceptions which may arise if: the *Offeree* does take action based on the offer, or in mutual agreement both parties agree silence is acceptance or prior dealings evidence silence was construed as acceptance, the court based on the preponderance of evidence before it might construe silence to be acceptance.

Question: What is the statute of limitations for a contract claim (i.e. if there is a breach, how many years can the injured party bring a suit)?

Answer: The prescribed period for contracts under **Sections 8 (1) (a)** and **12 (1) (a)** of the **Limitation Law of Lagos State** is six (6) years for simple contracts and twelve (12) years for contracts under seal (i.e.- made by way of a Deed).

Typically, most construction contracts are made by way of deed. A claim for breach of the contract must be commenced within 12 years from the date the event giving rise to the breach occurred. In the event that the construction contract is not made by way of a deed *i.e* a simple contract, the limitation period is 6 years.

Question: Are **Non-competes** and **Non-Disclosure Agreements (NDA)** enforceable?

Answer: Non-competition clauses can be enforced by courts. It is true that employers face an uphill battle in getting a judge to agree to enforce a non-compete, but it can and does happen. If you are wondering whether your non-compete will stick, ask an employment lawyer. The enforceability of a non-compete depends on the specifics of the wording of the clause itself and the overall employment contract. Some key considerations are whether the clause is clearly worded and whether it is limited in time, geography, and scope of what is covered. Typically, the court may weigh the inherent risk to the company vis-à-vis the employee's ability to make a living AND public good:

NDAs are enforceable if beyond the executed agreement you can show:

> a) existence of trade secret/confidential information;

b) that it was acquired improperly or as a result of the relationship; AND

c) that there was actual or threatened unauthorized use of the secret/ confidential information.

Advice & Tips:

- Attorneys can draft whatever you want, but always consider the legality and your ability to supervise/enforce your own agreement.

- Ambiguity is construed against the drafter, so evaluate your parameters of deciding who should draft a contract agreement for you. Always advise your attorney to use non-ambiguous words that they might have adopted to impress you. Insist that your contract agreement has a definition section where vague and reoccurring terms are defined clearly within the context of the agreement.

- Develop an exit strategy, should you need to repudiate a contract. If you are the non-breaching party, try communicating first (this may be relied on as evidence against the defaulting party), explore ADR options before a final recourse to a lawsuit.

- Be careful not to make promises you cannot commit to over emails. As a rule, be cautious of what you say over electronic platforms as the internet never forgets. It might be best to have an in-person meeting or a phone conversation prior to exchanging emails.

- A Contract Audit should be performed periodically to determine your outstanding rights and obligations. This gives you time to consider renegotiating some contract terms.

CHAPTER 3

Risks & Due Diligence

Aside from human resources, goods, services, and a few others, blue-chip companies thrive on two major fragile support systems; reputation and financial muscle. Reputation here includes goodwill and brand perception whereas asset base, share capital, liquid cash and other money's worth instruments constitutes its financial power. Therefore anything that can adversely impact the brand's public image and its profitability is considered as a risk. A third item to add to our cart of risks is legal risks. Brands don't want anything that may drag them to court or expose them to sanctions due to default to comply with regulations or for any other kind of wrongdoing. They usually prefer out of court settlement approach to disputes because litigation and other legal punitive measures affect the brand's reputation and finances negatively.

This brings us to the question, what is Risk? Merriam-Webster defines risk as "possibility of loss or injury" and I agree. In other words, anything that negatively impacts you or/and your business is a risk. That leads us to the next question, how do we avert or manage risks in Business?

You have to be able to identify, evaluate, and prioritize possible risks. Once you have been able to successfully pre-identify and assess possible risks, the next step is to build up your defense system to mitigate or manage them. Regardless of the strategy you choose to adopt, it should inculcate any or all of the following:

- Avoidance (eliminate, withdraw from or not become involved)

- Reduction (optimize – mitigate)
- Sharing (transfer – outsource or insure)
- Retention (accept and budget)

Do note that these risks can be intertwined in themselves and not mutually exclusive.

However, because of the immeasurable worth of reputation and the near impossibility of retrieving when lost, leading brands do everything in their power to protect their name even if it means losing all the monies. Hence according to the Holy Book, a good name is better than riches.

Legal Risks

Legal risk can be partly construed to mean the risk of financial or reputational loss that can result from lack of awareness or misunderstanding of, ambiguity in, or reckless indifference to, the way law and regulation apply to your business, its relationships, processes, products, and services. This includes but not limited to contract risks, regulatory risks, dispute risks, non-compliance risks, revocation of license risks and, so on.

There are steps you can take to protect yourself and business from legal risks. These steps are not in any way exhaustive but a fraction of a robust risk management strategy checklist.

1. *Pre-transaction Due Diligence*

Because we are in a world where most times nothing is as it seems, it necessitates the need to investigate and verify claims. Due diligence is an investigation, assessment, search, or review performed to confirm the facts of a matter under consideration. In the business world, due diligence requires an examination of all claims before entering into a proposed transaction with another party. Carrying out due diligence exercise is not negotiable if we mean business in mitigating risks. Again, this is where you need the services of a lawyer or a professional accustomed to the field in question.

2. Periodic Legal Audit

Most people including lawyers go to sleep when they have fulfilled pre-transaction due diligence, but that is where the real work starts with periodic legal audit. These include checking to ascertain that duties are being discharged as at when due, rights are not being infringed, terms of agreement are being adhered to, processes are being complied with and no introduction of encumbrances or vitiating factors. You may also choose to audit your company by undertaking an analysis of current operations, strategies, assets, and legal infrastructure in place. It may also include reviews of documentation procedures as well as employee policies. Often, this type of audit is intended to analyze a company's legal needs as well as to determine what those needs might be in the future. Likewise, it can be used to evaluate changes in legal requirements and new risks that may stem from changes to policies, objectives, or business structures.

3. **Compliance with laws and terms of agreements**

One of the ways to avoid risks is to comply. It pays to be compliant. A great percentage of the troubles that businesses run into is as a result of non-compliance with laid out regulations or industry best practices. The same applies to contracts and other legal relationships; except for frustration (an act of God), hardly will there be a breach of contract agreement if all the parties comply with the terms of engagement.

4. Continuous legal education
especially on rights and duties

Don't let Law intimidate you; even lawyers do not know all the laws. One of the brightest minds in the English Legal system by the name Lord Denning is often quoted saying *"God forbid that a lawyer knows all the law, but a good lawyer is one who knows where to find the law."* You too should be able to find the laws on your area of business and interest and continually abreast yourself with its provisions especially as it relates to your rights and duties. Lawyers respect enlightened clients who know what they know, ignorance can be expensive. Ignorance is a risk.

Challenge Assignment

Tunde Mustafa Obi (TMO) approaches **Mr. Ben Dover** of Citi-Zenith Bank for a credit facility of One Million USD ($1million) to revamp the IT infrastructure of his transport logistic company *TMO Delivery Ltd with share capital and assets valued to the tune of Five Hundred thousand USD ($500k)*. In his request letter, he claims to be the rightful owner of all that property known as TMO Plaza at #15 Sambisa Road, Owerri, Oyo State, and wishes to use same asset to use to secure the loan. As part of his equity contribution to the credit facility, he is laying claim to the Hundred thousand USD ($100k) in the account of one *Mr. Tolu Mustafa Obi* in Citi-Zenith Bank, whom he claims to be his late father who died of Covid-19 complications and left him as beneficiary and Next of Kin. Rumor has it that TMO is into illegal minining of diamond in Onitsha and money laundering. He has been accused by his political opponents of funding terrorism in Banana Island in order to destabilize the present government.

Question 1:

Identify all the possible risks that could arise from this transaction?

Question 2:

Identify all the steps you should take as **Mr. Ben Dover** to avert risks?

Case Study 2

2 Months Later...

*TMO receives an email from **Mr. Ben Dover** of Citi-Zenith Bank with an attached draft **term loan agreement** for his execution (signature). TMO was over excited about the new development but decided to consult you to advise him on what to do, haven learnt that you just graduated from **Tekedia Mini-MBA**?*

Question 1:

What will you advise TMO to look out for while reviewing a contract agreement?

TMO should review the contract document while looking out to:

- Identifying all parties properly
- Making sure all terms are defined
- Including necessary signature blocks
- Identify every referenced exhibits **(exhibit)**, schedules, etc. and making sure they are included
- Double checking all mathematical formulations
- Ensuring that the term expiration is explained
- Including instructions for early termination if applicable
- Identifying the rights of all parties in regards to the terms of the contract
- Checking that all of the performance obligations are accurate
- Verifying the accuracy of payment terms
- Clarifying any expenses that are reimbursable and how to go about it
- Verifying the accuracy of warranties and representations
- Verifying for indemnification
- Checking to see if insurance is required or should be
- Checking for boilerplate provisions

- Agreeing to governing law and legal jurisdiction
- Verifying provisions for attorney fees

Some other kind of agreements may include:

- Checking for a well-drafted NDA provision
- Verifying the presence of a non-compete and non-solicitation
- Checking who will own intellectual property

Advice & Tips: Exit strategy

For Lawyers: It is important to plan for the event that a client may want to get out of the contract, make sure there is appropriate language in their defining the terms and process for exiting the contract.

Every claim should be investigated and verified in the appropriate government registry if applicable. Claim of death- probate registry; title to property- Land Registry; claim of company- Corporate Affairs Commission; and so on. Don't just affirm or deny claims informally, provide your client with a detailed search report.

CHAPTER 4

Dispute Resolution

S till on risks and the need to protect yourself and business interest, one of the preemptive steps you may wish to take is to agree on a dispute resolution strategy prior to executing any high net worth contract or forging any legal relationship.

Dispute resolution fundamentally can be categorized into two major parts, the traditional and the alternative dispute resolution (ADR) process. Ironically what we now have as the traditional process (e.g. - the court system) used to be the alternative thousands of years ago; and what we have refined as the alternative used to be very informal and traditional. As what goes around keeps coming around we may end up having the ADR processes becoming traditional and our court systems revert to ADR.

In a bid not to confuse you further let me describe the term simply as a number of processes that can be used to resolve a conflict, dispute, or claim. As established above dispute resolution can be divided into two major categories:

- Adjudicative processes, such as litigation in which a judge or jury determines the outcome of a matter. OR
- Consensual processes, such as collaborative law, arbitration, mediation, conciliation, or negotiation, in which the parties attempt to reach an agreement.

The latter is an area that has become more attractive for businesses in order to preserve relationships, save time, and sometimes money. Permit me to refer to it as ADR, which can be partly defined as a means of settling an issue without going to court. ADR includes dispute resolution processes and techniques that act as a means for disagreeing parties to come to an agreement without exploring the option of litigation. Common forms of ADR include but not limited to:

- Conciliation
- Mediation

- Arbitration
- Negotiation
- Neutral evaluation
- Collaborative law
- Settlement Conferences (*known as Pre-trial conference in Nigeria*)

Due to constraint of time and space, we will just focus on Arbitration which is commonly seen in legal agreements under the Arbitration Clause. Arbitration is a form of alternative dispute resolution where parties agree not to take their dispute to court. Instead, they agree to resolve the dispute by hiring an arbitrator(s) to hear both sides and make a decision which is expected to be binding. By agreeing in advance to arbitration, the parties are waiving their constitutional right to the adjudicatory services of a court of competent jurisdiction. Typically, the arbitration decision is meant to be legally binding and not appealable, except in the very rare occurrence of fraud or other similar act on the part of the arbitrator.

Arbitration is often used in labor disputes, business, and social disputes because of its flexibility and informality. It **may** save you time, money, and sometimes business relationships to explore Arbitration or other ADR processes before heading to court. However, do not let anyone deceive you into thinking that Arbitration is always cheaper, faster and preserves relationships as that is not always true.

The following are some benefits of arbitration:

- Cost to the parties is **often** moderate compared to litigation in court.
- Some organizations that provide arbitration offer sliding fee schedules based on the size of the claim.
- It is a semi-informal procedure, and the rules of evidence are relaxed.
- There is speed and efficiency in the process.
- The proceedings are presumed to be confidential and private.
- The parties may control the process and procedure.
- Parties may choose to be represented by counsel.
- Informal investigation is allowed and Parties may agree on exchanging documents.
- The parties have the ability to select the arbitrator(s).

- If the parties are unable to agree on an arbitrator, the court or arbitration association may be asked to assist in the process.
- Parties can select an arbitrator with expertise in a certain subject matter.
- There is no jury and the arbitrator makes the final decision.

The following are some downsides of arbitration:

- Antagonism remains between the parties involved in the dispute.

- There is lack of full range of discovery.
- There is limited cross-examination of witnesses.
- Arbitration fees may be substantial, particularly in complex cases.
- Arbitrators typically make awards without written opinions or explanatory documents.
- Arbitration is the most formal type of alternative dispute resolution.
- Arbitrators sometimes "split the difference" when making an award, which may not be a desirable solution.
- It is either impossible or difficult to appeal an arbitration decision.

- Punitive damages are usually unlikely to be granted.

Advice & Tips:

Did you know that an arbitration award can be entered as a court judgment after being confirmed by a court of competent jurisdiction? Consult your attorney and further secure yourself.

CHAPTER 5

Labour and Employment

For starters, Labor and Employment law is a broad subject that deals chiefly with employer and employee relationships, unions, and other stakeholders. Even if you are a trader, entrepreneur or, a consultant, you might find something of interest under this topic.

As a legally recognized employee of a company, you have certain rights and laws in place to ensure your safety and fair treatment when working for companies operating in ~~the~~ Nigeria. You have probably come across them in your employee handbook (which most of us don't get to read) or at some point signed statements indicating you have received a copy of them. The next paragraph may come as shock to you, fasten your seat belt.

The *Nigerian Labour Act* which is the primary legislation that regulates the relationship between employers and employees is not applicable to all classes of employees in Nigeria. The Act uses the word 'workers' in describing employees, and defines workers as **not including** persons exercising administrative, executive, technical, or professional functions as public officers or otherwise. This suggests that if the nature of your role is administrative, executive, technical, or professional, you might not be covered by the Act. The Labour Act only covers employees engaged under a contract of **manual labour** or **clerical work** in the private and public sector. *Section 91* of the *Labour Act* defines a "worker," for purposes of the Labour Act, as:

"... *any person who has entered into or works under a contract with an employer, whether the contract is for manual labour, or clerical work or is expressed or implied or oral or written, and whether it is a contract of service or a contract personally to execute any work or labour ....*"

It is pertinent to note the exclusion of "*persons exercising administrative, executive, technical or professional functions as public officers or otherwise*", from the ambit of the Labour Act. So what happens to the excluded category which I assume most professionals fall under? Terms of employment of such excluded categories of employees are governed by the terms and conditions contained in their respective individual contracts of employment. This brings us back to contract, as the principles governing general contract agreements will also apply to contract of employment.

Therefore, we will focus on *a* few highlights of the Nigerian Labour law and allied matters.

Forced Labour

Do note that it is illegal to force anyone to work against their will. It is every Nigerian's right to be free from forced labour, and this right is guaranteed under the 1999 constitution. Apart from existing in the constitution, it is also restated in the Labour Act. Therefore, if you are being forced to work against your will, you can report to the police as it is a crime. However, the Labour Act gives the government the ability to requisition people to work during an emergency or a calamity, and this will not be classed as 'forced labour'.

Written Contract

Despite recognizing the various ways of establishing an employment contract, section 7 of the Labour Act still asserts that an employer must give an employee a written contract within 3 months of the commencement of the employment. The contract must have certain key terms – name of employer/employee, nature of employment, duration, wages etc. The essence is to ensure that the employee is protected by all the relevant terms being reduced to writing so the employee is abreast of his rights and duties. Also important is that if there is any change in the terms of the employment, it should be made known in writing to the employee within 1 month.

Wages

Any contract where the whole or part of the worker's wages is made payable in any other manner apart from legal tender shall be illegal, null, and void. Therefore, it is illegal for your employer to attempt to pay you with things other than money. A few other key things to note around wages are:

- It is illegal for any contract to be for the payment of wages at intervals exceeding one month unless with the written consent of the State Authority. This means if your employer makes you sign an employment contract where the employee is to be paid every quarter or every 6 weeks etc., such a contract is illegal.

- No employer can impose any restrictions as to the place and manner in which the employee can spend his/her wages. So your employer can't insist that you only buy lunch from the office canteen.
- Employers are not allowed to provide an advance of wages in excess of 1month wages.

Salary Deductions

Employers are not allowed to deduct an employee's wages for any reason, unless reasonable deduction for injury/loss caused to the employer by the employee, but only with prior written consent of an authorised labour officer. Also, if mistakenly you are overpaid, then you should know that the money which was overpaid can only be deducted within 3 months from the date of the overpayment. Any attempt by your employer to deduct the overpayment from your future salary after the expiration of this 3-month period is illegal.

Trade union membership

No employment contract can prevent workers from joining trade unions, and any contract which makes it a condition of employment that the worker should relinquish membership of a trade union or prejudices workers by reason of trade union membership is illegal.

Rest Hours, Sick Leave, and Holidays.
If a worker is at work for more than 6 hours a day, he/she must be given at least 1 hour of rest-interval in that day. Further, in every period of 7 days, a worker is entitled to at least 1 day of rest which must not be less than 24 consecutive hours. Every worker is also entitled to 12 days' sick leave for temporary illness certified by a registered medical practitioner. In addition, every employee after 12 months of continuous service is entitled to a holiday with full pay of at least 6 working days (this is exclusive of all the public holidays).

Maternity and Paternity leave
All female employees are entitled to at least 12 weeks' maternity leave with full pay. Unfortunately, the Nigerian Labour Act does not recognise paternity leave and makes no such provisions. However, in Lagos State, civil servants are entitled to 10

days' paternity leave within the first 2 months of the birth of the baby.

Transfer of employment
An employee must consent to the transfer of his/her employment from one employer to another for it to be valid, and the transfer must be endorsed by an authorised Labour officer. So if for instance your company is taken over by another company, your employment will not automatically move to this new company (employer) without first consulting you and getting your agreement to transfer your employment.

Termination of employment
With respect to the termination of an employment contract, the Labour Act provides for minimum notice period as follows:

- Where the employee has been employed for a period of 3 months or less, either party may terminate the contract with a minimum of 1-day notice
- Where the employee has been employed for a period of 3 months but less than 2 years, either party may terminate the contract with a minimum of 1-week notice

- where the employee has been employed for a period of 2 years but less than 5 years, either party may terminate the contract with a minimum of 2-weeks' notice
- Where the employee has been employed for a period of 5 years or more, either party may terminate the contract with a minimum of 1-month notice
- When giving notice of termination of employment contract where the notice is 1 week or more, the notice must be in writing.

CHAPTER 6

Business Ethics & Corporate Governance

Nigeria has lost 75 banks since the advent of banking in the country in 1914. Interestingly, the distress and eventual collapse of these banks were occasioned by factors relating to corporate governance. The banks did not collapse due to lack of customers or patronage but due to how they were managed and governed. For example, a study conducted by the Nigeria Deposit Insurance Corporation (NDIC) listed the factors that caused severe distress in these banks as follows: economic depression (25%), political crisis (17.9%), bad credit policy (25%), interference of board members (32.1%).

Law and ethics are not one and the same. Although law can encourage and guide ethical behaviour by laying out a framework, ethicists are of the view that law should be thought of as the bare minimum of an ethical framework. That further suggests that complying with the law and behaving ethically are not necessarily synonymous. For instance, law makes us understand that theft or fraudulent behaviour is illegal; but do not tell us that the series of questionable decisions that led to the fraud is illegal as well. That is where business ethics comes in, to guide the behaviour of corporations and influence management decisions positively.

One may be wondering, what in the world is the relationship between running a profitable business and corporate morality. Of a truth, we can't pretend that a fundamental objective of corporate governance isn't to increase shareholder value. However, successful corporations thrive within the society; to that end, they must maintain the values and norms of the society in which they operate. Therefore business ethics attempts to guide corporations through ethically difficult decisions.

The importance of business ethics reaches far beyond employee loyalty and morale, or the strength of a management team bond. As with all business initiatives, the ethical operation of a company is directly related to profitability in both the short and long term. The reputation of a business in the surrounding community, other businesses, and individual investors is paramount in determining whether a company is a worthwhile investment. If a company is perceived to not operate ethically, investors are less inclined to buy stock or otherwise support its operations.

Companies have more and more of an incentive to be ethical as the area of socially responsible and ethical investing keeps growing. The increasing number of investors seeking out ethically operating companies to invest in is driving more firms to take this issue more seriously. With consistent ethical behavior comes an increasingly positive public image, and there are few other considerations as important to potential investors and current shareholders. To retain a positive image, businesses must be committed to operating on an ethical foundation as it relates to the treatment of employees, respecting the surrounding environment, and fair market practices in terms of price and consumer treatment.

Most organizations can testify that they have noticed drastic reduction in fines, sanctions, law suites, negative press, conflict of interests, and internal fraud when they started prioritizing their commitment to corporate governance and complying with best practices. This leads us to our next topic.

CHAPTER 7

Company Secretarial Services

As you must have noticed there is so much expectation on a company from the society, shareholders, regulators, and other stakeholders. The daunting tasks of governance, managing risks, maintaining records, playing by the rules, and still remitting smiles to shareholders can be overwhelming. However, with an excellent company secretary, your company can be on auto cruise while you focus on your core objectives.

The company secretary is designed to be an administrator responsible for providing corporate secretarial services which include but not limited to legal and business advisory support. Despite the name, the role is not clerical or secretarial, though it might include providing administrative support. By virtue of *Section*

293 of the Companies and Allied Matters Act 2004 (CAMA), every company is required to have a company secretary.

There is no clear professional qualification mandated by CAMA in appointing a Company Secretary of a private company but in practice they adhere to the statutory standards set for a public company. These include:

    a. a member of the **Institute of Chartered Secretaries and Administrators**; **or**

    b. a legal practitioner within the meaning of the Legal Practitioners Act; **or**

    c. a member of the **Institute of Chartered Accountants of Nigeria** or such other bodies of accountants as are established from time to time by an Act; **or**

    d. any person who has held the office of the secretary of a public company for at least three years of the five years immediately preceding his appointment in a public company; **or**

e. a body corporate or firm consisting of members each of whom is qualified under paragraphs **(a)**, **(b)**, **(c)**, or **(d)** of this section.

If you are running a business in Nigeria, the company secretary post is one role that should be filled with the most qualified candidate. Whether you are a start-up or an offshore firm looking to penetrate the competitive business landscape of this bustling African business hub, investing in company secretarial services should be included in your playbook. The Company Secretary is like a prime minister to a state. S/he is the chief compliance officer, making sure that the company timely complies with all its regulatory obligations. Secretarial services obviate any possible operational risk for the business owners. Part of the duties includes but not limited to:

- Filing statutory reports and documents required to approve financial statements

- Maintaining and safeguarding the statutory registers and minute books of a company, including the Register of Directors, Register of Members, and company charter

- Initiating notices and correspondences for meetings and recording minutes
- Advising the board on regulatory and compliance related issues
- Carrying out such other administrative and support functions as may be directed by the directors of the company.

CHAPTER 8

Intellectual Property

Intellectual property (IP) is a multifaceted subject, which makes it complicated to know where to start. Here you can find attempted answers to some of the most common questions asked. For a detailed legal advice, consult an IP lawyer.

Frequently Asked Questions
What is intellectual property?

Based on the view of the World Intellectual Property Organization (WIPO) IP is a product of the mind which includes: inventions, literary and artistic works, any symbols, names, images, and designs used in commerce. Be careful to note the distinction between IP and IPRs (intellectual property rights). IPRs are legal forms of protection for IP and fall into four main areas: patent, copyright, trademark and design rights. Sometimes the common law right against *passing off* is construed to be a distinct part of the list.

Why is this important to me?

If you generate IP that you wish to protect and which you think might be able to be exploited for some benefit, you may want to consider how to legally protect your rights and what rights you already have. Further, you need to also realise that others have rights as well, e.g. anyone with whom you have collaborated or in whose work you have been involved (employer) may have an interest in any IP generated as a result of this work and anyone whose work you use needs to be referenced appropriately.

What can I protect?

- The way a product works: **PATENTS**
- The way a product looks: **REGISTERED DESIGNS**
- What a product is called: **TRADEMARKS**
- What a product says: **COPYRIGHT**

What is Patentable?

- New products;
- Improved parts and features of products;
- New or improved methods and processes;

- New uses of known things;
- Software – This is only patentable if claiming a technical effect.

Which countries are covered by my patent?

- The country where the patent is granted.
- If for instance, you want protection in other countries in Europe, you need to file further applications through the *European Patent Convention* (**EPC**), the *Patent Cooperation Treaty* (**PCT**) or individually if the countries that you seek protection in do not belong to either the EPC or the PCT.

CHAPTER 9

5G of Retainer Arrangement

When someone threatens to call their lawyer, he or she could very well have a lawyer "on retainer." To have a lawyer on retainer means that the client pays a lawyer an agreed amount periodically. In return, the lawyer performs some legal services whenever the client needs them. Retainers are most useful for businesses that need constant legal work but do not have enough money to hire a lawyer full time to work in-house or need external lawyers to support their full time in-house legal team. Also, individuals are likely to need a lot of legal work and might want to have a lawyer or law firm on retainer.

A retainer arrangement benefits both the client and the attorney. The attorney has the assurance of being paid monthly or at least regularly. This is particularly helpful if a client is slow in paying. On the other hand the retainer arrangement is also beneficial for the client because it provides priority attention and an estimated budget for legal fees. Depending on the nature of your case, however, it's not uncommon for a legal matter to "blow up," requiring much more time and effort to resolve.

Before you say "I do"

What do you look out for before jumping into the hands of a lawyer? It's unfortunate to observe how people choose lawyers based on family, religious, and social ties without paying attention to their area of expertise. Some companies have lost lawsuits and hard earned money due to the incompetence of their legal arsenal. That a lawyer is fluent in legalese and is well known doesn't mean s/he is suited for you. S/he has to be well known in your area of need. For the records, no lawyer is an expert in every area of law and as such you have to give it some thoughts before saying "I do".

This brings us to what I intentionally couched as the **5G** of a retainer agreement. It simply means five things I feel you should include in your checklist when shopping for a lawyer.

Grades

If you are settling for an individual lawyer it might be wise to ask for the person's resume/CV and ascertain the person's grades among other things. It may not be a perfect pointer to who the person is as people change, but it may give you some first impressions and presumptions to work with. If for instance your candidate graduated with a 3rd class it could be a red flag upon which other presumptions of negligence, ineptitude and mediocrity are built, though this is not always the case. That is why it is a presumption, a very rebuttable presumption at that, and not a flawless conclusion. On the other extreme, if the candidate finished with a 1st Class, it could be a pointer to their diligence and commitment to tasks and excellence as hardly do people bag a first class by chance. Again, people change and nothing is as it seems- so I advocate you give everyone a clean slate and a chance to prove you right or wrong.

When it comes to law firms, research on how they are graded alongside other firms. You can't be working on a $100m facility and you are shopping for a road side law firm that has no experience in project finance and *un-googleable*. Institutions such as IFLR 1000 and Chambers Global tell you more about top law firms doing exceptionally well in every jurisdiction.

Growth

While holding that resume, assess the candidate's growth trajectory post call. What has S/he been doing since graduation till date? If they have never worked for a law firm it could mean that all they know is based on all they have experienced and might have never leveraged on the knowledge and experiences of veterans in the profession. Check if the candidate(s) has been committed to continuous personal development since graduation, do they have post graduate degree, a certification in a different field, are there publications credited to their names?

Groups

Just like Liverpool FC fans lawyers weren't designed to walk alone. Lawyers are meant to be interdependent, so find out if they belong to the Bar Society/Association of their jurisdiction. You can also go ahead to investigate if they are in good standing and have active membership. Belonging to other professional associations, networks, social and volunteer groups could be a plus.

For law firms, check their legal team; review their individual profiles on their website, or look them up on LinkedIn. Check out for their reviews on social media as well as followership, it reveals a lot.

Gift

It is very important to pay attention to their gifting, which is their area of expertise. Again, this is where LinkedIn comes in handy and views from referrals. You have to make sure that your prospective attorney has the requisites skill set and network needed to deliver on your tasks within the provided time, quality and budget. When it comes to law suits, reviewing law reports will among other things give you an idea of lawyers and firms that are often featured in some matters.

Gig

Finally, what is their current gig? Have they been keeping busy? If they are not busy it could be a blunt pointer that they don't know what they are doing as the result for good work is more work. Again, probe and keep probing till you are satisfied.

Retainer Fee

Pre-agree with your attorney before signing a retainer agreement. Let the scope of work be defined and the payment arrangement. Whether it is a contingency fee, flat fee or even hourly rates, you should pre-agree before signing and when you do be honorable enough to comply. However, be sure there are no hidden charges.

CHAPTER 10

Future of Business Law

As you might have noticed businesses are beginning to streamline their expenses and adopting different cost cutting measures to stay profitable. It is no longer news that jobs will be lost to robots and that current AI disruption that is flushing out unskilled labour is now coming for highly skilled roles.

For instance, most entrepreneurs do not consult lawyers to prepare basic contract documents for them anymore, they just go on Google and download a template which they might tweak to meet their need. Guess what? That wouldn't make it less admissible as evidence in court.

The courts also are relaxing their rules and procedures as well as birthing innovation in the way trials are conducted. Recall that the Borno State High Court of Nigeria (No. 13) has blazed the trail of recording the first virtual court session in the country on the 27th of April, 2020 wherein the presiding judge, *Hon. Justice Fadawu Umaru* discharged and acquitted the accused in *State Vs Aliyu* of Culpable Homicide punishable with death. This may translate to an attorney getting a major slash on his appearance fee and the client saving some more money.

I foresee with growing unlimited access to legal texts online and court relaxing the technicalities associated with trial, clients may begin to research their matters and defend their suits in e-courts by themselves. Currently, Corporate Affairs Commission (CAC) of Nigeria has relaxed some of their procedures, accommodating anyone to register their business name without recoursing to the services of a lawyer.

It is gradually becoming a *Do-it-yourself* age as what a lawyer can do, you can do better. In the future it seems to me the more abreast you are with laws and where to find them, the leaner your legal budget may shrink. To save more, learn more.

Conclusion

We have come to the end of our time together and I hope you had a fantastic time and you received immense value for it. At this point, you should have a basic understanding of business law and how it affects you and your business. There is more to business law than what we have discussed above. Should you have further questions and would like to learn more, feel free to reach me on <u>emekambah2@yahoo.com</u>

References:

1. https://www.upcounsel.com/how-to-review-contracts
2. https://www.ey.com/Publication/vwLUAssets/ey-legal-risk-2-show-you-are-in-control/$FILE/ey-legal-risk-2-show-you-are-in-control.pdf
3. https://www.wisegeek.com/what-is-a-legal-audit.htm
4. https://www.upcounsel.com/how-to-review-contracts
5. https://en.wikipedia.org/wiki/Dispute_resolution
6. https://www.allbusiness.com/pros-and-cons-of-arbitration-4128-1.html
7. https://lawpadi.com/9-things-every-nigerian-know-labour-act/
8. https://docksci.com/corporate-governance-and-business-ethics_5a230dabd64ab24b88e83c64.html
9. https://www.investopedia.com/ask/answers/040815/why-are-business-ethics-important.asp
10. http://www.hgf.com/faq/
11. https://www.gla.ac.uk/media/Media_391396_smxx.pdf

12. https://hirealawyer.findlaw.com/attorney-fees-and-agreements/what-does-it-mean-to-have-a-lawyer-on-retainer.html
13. https://www.thebalancesmb.com/hiring-an-attorney-on-retainer-398441
14. https://allafrica.com/stories/2007111905 60.html

About the Author

Chukwuemeka Mbah is an international corporate commercial lawyer (trained in both common law and civil law jurisdictions) with long standing interest in transactional law, energy, company secretarial services and corporate governance. With forte in legal advisory, negotiation, legal drafting and review, business development and client relationship management, Mbah can deliver on tasks within the provided time, quality and budget. He is based in North America but consults for African based *Centurion Law Group* and *Justice Quest Partners* as an on-demand Lawyer. Mbah can afford you 90 minutes of free consultation.

www.ingramcontent.com/pod-product-compliance
Lightning Source LLC
Chambersburg PA
CBHW061011260726
48661CB00005B/2152

overhead and look up .After a few breaths, hold the position and then exchange sides.

Triangle Pose (Trikonasana): Stand with your feet wide apart. While extending the other arm overhead, lower one arm to your shin or the ground. Keep your chest open and gaze towards the raised hand.

Seated Forward Bend (Paschimottanasana): Legs outstretched in front of you while you sit. Reach toward your toes while hinging at the hips. Hold this stretch for a few breaths, keeping your back straight.

Corpse Pose (Savasana): Lie flat on your back with your arms at your sides and your eyes closed. Relax completely, focusing on your breath and letting go of tension.

You can perform each of these poses for a few breaths, gradually increasing the duration as you become more comfortable. It is important to note that you must breathe deeply and mindfully throughout your morning yoga routine. When starting off, especially if you're a newbie, it's crucial to pay attention to your body and avoid overexerting yourself. As you gain more experience and flexibility, you can explore more advanced poses and longer routines.

30 SIMPLE MORNING YOGA EXERCISES

1. Mountain Pose (Tadasana): Mountain Pose is a foundational yoga pose that focuses on grounding and posture. Stand with your feet together, weight evenly distributed, and your arms by your sides. Keep your spine straight, shoulders relaxed, and your gaze forward. Breathe deeply and mindfully, feeling the connection between your feet and the earth.

2. Child's Pose (Balasana): Child's Pose is a resting and calming position Begin by kneeling on the floor, big toes touching and knees apart. Sit back on your heels and stretch your arms forward, lowering your torso to the ground. Rest your forehead on the mat, relax, and take deep, slow breaths. This pose gently stretches your lower back and hips.

3. Cat-Cow Stretch: This is a dynamic stretch that helps warm up the spine. Begin in a tabletop posture on your hands and knees. Inhale as you arch your back, lifting your head and tailbone (Cow Pose), and exhale as you round your back, tucking your chin (Cat Pose). Flow smoothly between these two poses for a few breaths, synchronizing your movements with your breath.

4. Downward Facing Dog (Adho Mukha Svanasana): Downward Dog is an energizing and rejuvenating pose that stretches the entire body. Start in a tabletop position and then lift your hips, straighten your legs, and press your palms into the ground. Your body will form an inverted V-shape. Push your heels towards the floor to stretch your hamstrings and calves. Keep your head relaxed and breathe deeply.

5. Warrior I (Virabhadrasana I): Warrior I is a strong standing pose that enhances strength and focus. Step forward with one foot and back with the other. Turn your back foot at a 45-degree angle. Bend your front knee to a 90-degree angle and raise your arms overhead, palms facing each other. Gaze up and breathe deeply.

6. Triangle Pose (Trikonasana): This pose stretches the sides of your body and improves balance. Stand with your legs wide apart, arms extended parallel to the ground. Reach down with one hand to your shin or the floor while extending the other arm up, creating a triangle shape with your body. Keep your chest open and gaze towards the raised hand.

7. Seated Forward Bend (Paschimottanasana): This pose is excellent for stretching the entire back of your body. Sit with your legs stretched and your toes contracted in front of you. Inhale, lengthen your spine, and exhale as you hinge at your hips, reaching for your toes. You can grab your shins, ankles, or feet. Keep your back straight, and avoid straining.

8. Corpse Pose (Savasana): Savasana is a relaxation pose that helps to integrate your practice. Lie flat on your back with your legs extended and your arms at your sides. Close your eyes, and consciously relax your entire body. Focus on your breath, letting go of tension and stress. Stay in this pose for a few minutes to rejuvenate your body and mind.

9. Bridge Pose (Setu Bandha Sarvangasana): Bridge Pose is a great pose for strengthening the back and glutes lie on your back with your knees bent and your feet hip-width apart. Put your arms at your sides, palms down.. On an inhale, press through your feet, lifting your hips off the ground. Keep your thighs and feet parallel. Interlace your fingers beneath your hips and press your arms and shoulders into the ground. Lift your chest towards your chin, and breathe deeply. Hold for a few breaths.

10. Happy Baby Pose (Ananda Balasana): Happy Baby Pose is a playful stretch for the hips and lower back. Lie on your back and raise your legs up to your sternum. Hold the outsides of your feet with your hands, keeping your feet flexed. Gently pull your knees towards the floor beside your ribs, creating the image of a happy baby. Relax and breathe deeply.

11. Upward Facing Dog (Urdhva Mukha Svanasana): This is a backbend that strengthens the back and opens the chest. Begin by lying down on your mat, face down. Place your hands on the floor beside your ribcage, fingers pointing forward. Inhale as you press into your palms, lifting your chest and thighs off the ground. Keep your legs straight and shoulders down, extending through the spine. Gaze forward and breathe deeply.

12. Cobra Pose (Bhujangasana): Cobra Pose is similar to upward facing Dog but with the lower body on the ground. Start by lying face down with your hands under your shoulders. Inhale, gently lift your head and chest off the mat, keeping your elbows slightly bent. Your pelvis and legs should remain on the ground. Breathe deeply and arch your back gently.

13. Puppy Pose (Uttana Shishosana): Puppy Pose is a gentle stretch for the back and shoulders. Start in a tabletop position. Walk forward with your hands while maintaining your hips above your knees. Reduce your chest and forehead to the carpet. Your arms should be extended, and your hips should be above your knees. Relax in this position and breathe deeply.

14. Camel Pose (Ustrasana): Camel Pose is a heart-opening pose that stretches the front of the body. Kneel with your knees hip-width apart. Tuck your toes under or keep them flat on the mat Place your hands on your lower back, with your fingers pointing down. Inhale as you arch your back, leaning back and reaching for your heels. Keep your chest lifted and your neck relaxed. Breathe deeply and hold the pose for a few breaths.

15. Low Lunge (Anjaneyasana): Low Lunge is a deep hip flexor stretch that helps improve flexibility and balance. Start in Downward Dog, and step one foot forward between your hands. Lower your back knee to the ground, keeping your front knee directly above your ankle. Keep your hands on the floor or raise your arms overhead. Breathe deeply and notice how your hip flexors stretch.

16. Boat Pose (Navasana): Boat Pose is a core-strengthening pose Sit on the floor with your legs outstretched. Lean back slightly, keeping your back straight. Balance on your sit bones and lift your feet off the ground. Keep your legs and torso at a 45-degree angle to the floor. You can keep your arms extended forward or hold onto the backs of your thighs. Engage your core and breathe deeply.

17. Extended Triangle Pose (Utthita Trikonasana): This is a side stretch that also improves balance and flexibility. Stand with your legs wide apart. Extend your arms parallel to the ground. Reach down with one hand to your shin, ankle, or the floor, while extending the other arm up. Keep your chest open and gaze towards the raised hand. Breathe deeply, feeling the stretch along your side body.

18. Half Pigeon Pose (Ardha Kapotasana): Half Pigeon Pose is a deep hip opener. Start in a lunge position with one leg forward. Slide your front foot towards the opposite wrist, lowering your shin to the ground. You should stretch your back leg behind you. Sit upright and breathe deeply, feeling the stretch in your hip.

19. Plank Pose: Plank Pose is a core-strengthening pose that also works the arms and shoulders. Begin in a push-up position with your arms straight, wrists below your shoulders, and your body in a straight line. Engage your core and maintain a strong, straight back. Breathe deeply and hold this pose, working on your strength and stability.

20. Chair Pose (Utkatasana): Chair Pose is a standing pose that strengthens the legs and core. Begin in Mountain Pose. On an inhale, raise your arms overhead. On an exhale, bend your knees as if sitting in an imaginary chair. You should stretch your back leg behind you. Breathe deeply and hold this pose, feeling the burn in your quadriceps.

21. Tree Pose (Vrikshasana): Tree Pose is a balance pose that also helps improve focus and stability. Stand on one foot and bring the sole of your other foot to your inner thigh or calf, avoiding the knee. Put your hands in a prayer stance at your heart. Focus your gaze on a fixed point to help with balance. Breathe deeply and hold, then switch sides.

22. Thread the Needle Pose: Thread the Needle is a gentle shoulder and upper back stretch Begin in a tabletop posture on your hands and knees. Slide one arm underneath the other, lowering your shoulder and ear to the ground. Rest in this twisted position, feeling the stretch in your upper back. Breathe deeply and switch sides.

23. Fish Pose (Matsyasana): Fish Pose is a heart-opening pose that also stretches the neck and throat. Lie on your back with your legs stretched out. Place your hands beneath your hips, palms down. On an inhale, lift your chest and arch your back, allowing the top of your head to rest on the ground. Keep your elbows tucked in and breathe deeply.

24. Supine Spinal Twist: Supine Spinal Twist is a gentle twist that releases tension in the lower back and hips Lie down on your back, knees bent. Extend your arms out to the sides in a T position. Drop your knees to one side as your shoulders remain on the ground. Look in the opposite direction of your knees. Breathe deeply, feeling the twist in your spine, and then switch sides.

25. Extended Hand-to-Big-Toe Pose (Utthita Hasta Padangusthasana): This is a balance pose that also improves hamstring flexibility. Stand in Mountain Pose. Lift one leg and hold the big toe with your hand. Extend the leg forward and then to the side while keeping your chest open. Breathe deeply and maintain your balance, then switch legs.

26. Upward Plank Pose (Purvottanasana): Upward Plank is a backbend that strengthens the arms and shoulders. Sit with your legs extended and your hands behind you, fingers pointing towards your feet. Lift your hips off the ground on an inhalation. Keep your feet flexed and your chest open. Breathe deeply and hold the pose.

27. Garland Pose (Malasana): Garland Pose is a squatting pose that stretches the hips and groin. Begin in a squat with your feet wider than hip-width apart and your toes turned slightly outward. Bring your hands to your heart in a prayer position, pressing your elbows against your knees. Breathe deeply and hold the squat, feeling the stretch in your hips.

28. Camel Ride Pose (Ushtrasana): Camel Ride Pose is a variation of Camel Pose that provides a deep backbend. Kneel with your knees hip-width apart. Tuck your toes under or keep them flat on the mat. Put your hands on your lower back with your fingers pointing down. On an inhale, arch your back, leaning back and reaching for your heels. Keep your chest lifted and your neck relaxed. Breathe deeply and hold the pose.

29. Legs Up the Wall Pose (Viparita Karani): This is a restorative pose that promotes relaxation. Sit with your side against a wall. While resting on your back, swing your legs up the wall. Your buttocks should be close to the wall, and your legs extended upward. Close your eyes and breathe deeply as you relax your arms at your sides.. This pose is excellent for reducing stress and promoting relaxation.

30. Shoulder Stand (Sarvangasana):

Shoulder Stand is an advanced inversion that promotes circulation and relaxation. Lie on your back with your legs stretched out. Lift your legs overhead, supporting your lower back with your hands. Your body should be in a straight line, and your toes should point toward the ceiling. Breathe deeply and hold this inversion. This pose should be practiced with caution and under the guidance of a yoga instructor, especially if you're a beginner.

These are 30 simple morning yoga exercises with detailed explanations. Remember to practice at your own pace, listen to your body, and gradually build your flexibility and strength over time. Yoga can be a wonderful way to start your day with mindfulness and relaxation.

MORNING YOGA THAT REDUCES WEIGHT

Sun Salutations (Surya Namaskar)

Sun Salutations are a foundational and dynamic series of 12 yoga postures performed in a graceful flow. They serve as an invigorating way to awaken the body, stimulate circulation, and increase overall flexibility. Sun Salutations encourage deep breathing and concentration as you transition through poses, promoting a profound sense of mindfulness. Over time, these movements enhance muscle tone, boost metabolism, and contribute to weight loss by raising the heart rate and increasing calorie burn. Practicing Sun Salutations regularly in the morning not only promotes physical fitness but also creates a positive and focused mindset for the day ahead.

This specialized class is designed with weight management in mind, offering dynamic poses and sequences that elevate the heart rate and increase calorie expenditure. It blends elements of strength, flexibility, and endurance to provide a well-rounded workout. By targeting key muscle groups and promoting cardiovascular health, Yoga for Weight Loss can help individuals shed excess pounds and maintain a healthy body weight.

Power Yoga: Power yoga is a vigorous and athletic

form of yoga that combines strength, flexibility, and stamina. It involves a fast-paced series of poses, offering an effective cardiovascular workout that helps with calorie burn and muscle toning. The continuous flow of challenging postures challenges the body, promoting overall fitness and weight loss.

Vinyasa Flow: Vinyasa Flow yoga emphasizes the synchronization of breath with movement, offering a fluid and dynamic practice. As you transition from one pose to another, this style elevates heart rate, engages various muscle groups, and burns calories. It improves cardiovascular fitness, promotes flexibility, and can significantly aid in weight management.

Ashtanga Yoga: Ashtanga Yoga is a structured and demanding yoga practice that centers on strength, endurance, and flexibility. By following a specific sequence of postures, individuals can build lean muscle mass, enhance metabolism, and ultimately support weight loss.

Hot Yoga (Bikram or Hot Vinyasa)

Hot yoga is practiced in a room with elevated temperatures, leading to increased sweating and detoxification. The combination of challenging poses and a heated environment enhances flexibility, strengthens the core, and promotes calorie burn. This practice can help individuals shed pounds, release toxins, and improve overall health.

Core Yoga: Core-focused yoga sessions are designed to strengthen the abdominal muscles, leading to improved posture and aiding in weight management. A strong core supports the spine and creates a leaner appearance. Core yoga targets these muscles, contributing to a more toned physique and enhanced overall fitness.

Kundalini Yoga: Kundalini yoga combines dynamic postures, breathing exercises, and meditation to promote mental clarity and emotional balance. This decreases stress, which helps prevent emotional overeating and, as a result, aids in weight management. Through the awakening of inner energy, individuals can develop a healthier relationship with food and enhance overall well-being.

Aerial Yoga: Aerial yoga introduces the use of a hammock that allows for a unique and challenging yoga experience. The hammock engages core muscles and promotes overall strength. As you perform various poses suspended in the air, you enhance flexibility and strength, which can contribute to weight loss.

Cardio Yoga: Some yoga classes incorporate cardio elements like jumping or fast-paced sequences. By elevating the heart rate and increasing calorie burn, cardio yoga supports weight loss. This combination of traditional yoga with cardio exercises creates an effective full-body workout that promotes cardiovascular health and muscle engagement.

These detailed explanations provide insights into how each morning yoga practice can contribute to physical fitness and weight management. The comprehensive understanding of these practices allows individuals to make informed choices about which style aligns best with their goals and preferences for their morning yoga routine.

Pilates Yoga Fusion: The fusion of yoga and Pilates creates a dynamic practice that blends the flexibility and mindfulness of yoga with the core-strengthening benefits of Pilates. This combination results in a full-body workout that promotes calorie burn, muscle engagement, and enhanced physical fitness. As the practice targets both flexibility and core strength, it helps individuals develop a leaner physique, which is beneficial for weight management.

Jivamukti Yoga: Jivamukti Yoga is a holistic approach to yoga that integrates yoga philosophy with a physically demanding practice. By emphasizing strength, flexibility, and endurance, it supports overall fitness. Jivamukti also encourages mindfulness and self-awareness, creating a sense of balance and well-being. This mindfulness can lead to better choices, such as healthier eating habits, which ultimately contribute to weight management.

Budokon Yoga: Budokon is a fusion of yoga and martial arts principles. This practice enhances agility and strength while supporting weight management through engaging, high-energy movements. The combination of yoga and martial arts fosters physical fitness and mental clarity, contributing to overall well-being.

Yoga Sculpt: Yoga sculpt classes incorporate hand weights into the practice, creating a dynamic full-body workout. The added resistance from weights promotes muscle development, calorie burn, and overall toning. Yoga sculpt enhances muscle engagement, supporting weight loss and offering a balanced approach to physical fitness.

CorePower Yoga: CorePower Yoga combines core-focused exercises with vinyasa flow. This style emphasizes abdominal strength and overall fitness. By targeting the core muscles, it promotes better posture and leaner physique, aiding in weight management. Additionally, the cardiovascular aspects of vinyasa flow help elevate the heart rate, contributing to calorie burn.

Sivananda Yoga: Sivananda Yoga follows a specific sequence of 12 basic postures and focuses on proper breathing and relaxation. While not an intense calorie-burning practice, it aids in stress management and mindfulness. Reducing stress is crucial for preventing emotional overeating, and the relaxation techniques incorporated in Sivananda Yoga can be helpful for weight management.

Shadow Yoga: Shadow Yoga combines elements of yoga and martial arts, fostering physical fitness and mindfulness. This practice promotes balance and well-being, which can aid in weight management. The engagement of various muscle groups and controlled movements contribute to overall physical fitness.

Yin-Yang Yoga: Yin-Yang Yoga is a practice that combines the meditative, passive qualities of Yin with the dynamic, active aspects of Yang yoga. This combination strikes a balance between relaxation and activity, promoting both mindfulness and physical fitness. The dynamic elements engage muscle groups and increase calorie burn, contributing to weight management.

Yoga HIIT (High-Intensity Interval Training): Yoga HIIT combines traditional yoga poses with high-intensity intervals. This practice elevates the heart rate and promotes calorie burn while enhancing flexibility and strength. It is an effective way to target weight loss through a balanced approach to physical fitness.

Interval Flow Yoga: Interval Flow Yoga alternates between intense bursts of activity and recovery periods. This approach engages different muscle groups, elevates the heart rate, and promotes weight loss. By including high-intensity intervals and periods of active recovery, it offers a well-rounded workout that enhances physical fitness.

These comprehensive explanations provide a deeper understanding of how each morning yoga practice can support weight management, physical fitness, and overall well-being. By exploring these different styles, individuals can select the practice that aligns most effectively with their goals and preferences, ensuring a productive and satisfying morning yoga routine.

HOW TO KNOW THE TYPE OF YOGA AS A BEGINNER

Clarify Your Goals:

Start by identifying your primary goals. Are you looking to increase flexibility, manage stress, build strength, or lose weight? Understanding your objectives will guide your choice.

Assess Your Fitness Level: Consider your current physical fitness level. If you are a beginner, it's important to choose a style that matches your fitness and flexibility.

Research Different Styles: Research the various types of yoga to get a sense of what each offers. Some popular options include Hatha, Vinyasa, Ashtanga, Bikram, Yin, and Kundalini, each with its own characteristics.

Consider Your Personality and Preferences: Think about your personality and what appeals to you. Are you drawn to vigorous, dynamic practices, or do you prefer gentle, meditative sessions? Choose a style that resonates with your desired preferences.

Try Different Classes: Experiment with different classes or online videos. Most yoga studios offer introductory classes or trial sessions. Attend a few to get a feel for the practice and the instructor's teaching style.

Talk to Instructors: Reach out to yoga instructors or studio staff and ask questions. They can provide insights into which style might suit you best based on your goals and physical abilities.

Consider Any Health Concerns: If you have specific health concerns or physical limitations, consult a healthcare professional or a yoga instructor. They can recommend styles that are safe and beneficial for you.

Evaluate Class Intensity: Determine the intensity level that suits you. Styles like Power Yoga and Ashtanga are more physically demanding, while Hatha and Yin are gentler options for beginners.

Think about Lifestyle and Schedule: Consider your daily routine and schedule. Some styles, like Hot Yoga, might require more time and preparation due to the heated environment.

Trust Your Intuition: Listen to your gut feeling. The style that resonates most with you is likely the one that will keep you motivated and coming back to your mat.

Combine Styles: Keep in mind that you can combine different styles of yoga in your practice. Many practitioners enjoy a mix of more vigorous styles with more restorative or meditative practices.

Seek Guidance from an Instructor: Don't hesitate to consult with a certified yoga instructor. They can provide personalized recommendations based on your specific goals and abilities.

Consider the Studio or Online Platform: If you prefer practicing in a studio, visit a few local yoga studios to get a sense of their atmosphere and the types of classes they offer. If you opt for online classes, explore various platforms to find those that align with your preferred style and instructor.

Assess Your Stress Levels: Think about your stress levels and mental well-being. If you're looking to reduce stress and promote relaxation, styles like Yin or Restorative yoga may be more suitable. These practices focus on deep stretching, gentle poses, and mindfulness.

Be Patient and Open-Minded: As a beginner, it's important to be patient with yourself. Yoga is a journey, and it's okay to start with a basic class and gradually progress to more advanced styles as you become more comfortable with the practice. Keep an open mind and allow yourself to explore and grow.

Join a Community: Consider joining a yoga community or group, whether in a studio, gym, or online. Being part of a supportive community can help you stay motivated and connected with like-minded individuals who share your interests and goals.

Take Trial Classes: Many studios offer trial classes or introductory packages that allow you to explore different styles before committing to a specific practice. Make use of these opportunities to get a firsthand experience.

Commit to Consistency: Once you find the style that resonates with you, commit to a regular practice. Consistency is key to experiencing the full benefits of yoga, whether you're aiming for increased flexibility, stress reduction, or overall well-being.

Be Open to Evolution: As you progress in your yoga journey, your preferences and goals may evolve. Stay open to trying different styles or intensities, as your needs and interests may change over time.

Selecting the right type of yoga as a beginner is a personal decision that should align with your goals, fitness level, and lifestyle. Remember that there is no one-size-fits-all approach, and it's perfectly acceptable to explore different styles until you discover the one that brings you the most joy and fulfillment. Yoga is a lifelong practice, and it's an opportunity to cultivate self-awareness, strength, and balance in both your body and mind.

Build a Strong Foundation: Starting with a style that focuses on the fundamentals can be incredibly beneficial for beginners. Hatha yoga, for example, places a strong emphasis on mastering basic postures, alignment, and breath control. This foundation will serve you well as you progress in your yoga journey.

Seek Inspiration and Guidance: Look for sources of inspiration that align with your goals and resonate with you. Books, podcasts, and online resources can provide valuable insights into different yoga styles, philosophies, and teachings. Additionally, many experienced practitioners and teachers share their knowledge on social media and personal blogs.

Explore Specialized Classes: Once you've gained confidence and experience in yoga, you might consider exploring more specialized classes. For example, prenatal yoga is tailored for expectant mothers, while seniors may benefit from chair yoga. These specialized classes can address unique needs and goals.

Listen to Your Body: Listening to your body is one of the most crucial components of yoga. If a particular style or pose doesn't feel right for you or causes discomfort, it's crucial to modify or explore alternatives. Never push yourself beyond your comfort level, and always prioritize safety and well-being.

Stay Open to Adaptation: Over time, your body and interests may change. Your choice of yoga style doesn't have to be fixed. Be open to adaptation, and explore different styles as your journey evolves.

Consider Private Instruction: If you're uncertain about which style is right for you, consider private lessons with a certified instructor. They can offer personalized guidance and tailor a practice to your specific needs and goals.

Find Balance in Your Practice: The most effective and fulfilling yoga practice is one that offers a balance between effort and ease. While certain styles may initially challenge you, it's essential to find a practice that brings you joy and encourages self-compassion. Your yoga practice should leave you feeling refreshed, centered, and at peace with yourself.

Seek Recommendations from Peers: Connect with friends, family, or colleagues who practice yoga and ask for their recommendations. They may have valuable insights based on their experiences and preferences.

Make Your Practice Your Own: Ultimately, your yoga journey is a deeply personal one. It's essential to make your practice your own. Whether you prefer a specific style, instructor, or home practice, the key is to find what resonates with you and brings you the most fulfillment and growth.

Choosing the right type of yoga as a beginner is an empowering and enriching process. As you embark on your yoga journey, note that the practice is not just about physical postures but also about nurturing your inner self and achieving holistic well-being. Be patient with yourself, stay open to exploration, and savor the transformative benefits of yoga that await you.

CONCLUSION

Embarking on a journey of simple morning yoga for beginners offers a beautiful opportunity to nurture your physical and mental well-being. It's a chance to greet each day with a fresh perspective, a calm mind, and a body that feels rejuvenated. The benefits of morning yoga extend beyond the physical realm, encompassing stress reduction, enhanced mindfulness, and a sense of inner peace.

As you explore the various types of morning yoga practices and find the one that resonates with you, remember that yoga is a deeply personal endeavor. It's not about competition or perfection; it's about progress and self-discovery. The poses and sequences can be tailored to your unique needs and preferences, ensuring a practice that fits seamlessly into your daily routine.

With consistency, dedication, and patience, you'll witness the transformation that morning yoga can bring into your life. You'll find that the stiffness of dawn gives way to the suppleness of sunrise, and your morning yoga practice becomes a cherished ritual.

Now, I encourage you to take the first step toward a healthier, more balanced life by incorporating morning yoga into your daily routine. Whether you're aiming to increase flexibility, reduce stress, tone your body, or simply start your day with a sense of calm, morning yoga is a path to wellness that welcomes all. Begin your journey today, and let the benefits of morning yoga enrich your life in ways you never imagined. Your yoga mat is your sanctuary, and your practice is your personal voyage of self-discovery.

So, rise with the sun, unroll your mat, and breathe in the tranquility of the morning. Embrace the transformative power of morning yoga for beginners, and watch as it brings a new sense of vitality, balance, and harmony into your life.

Begin your morning yoga journey now.

Happy reading!!!

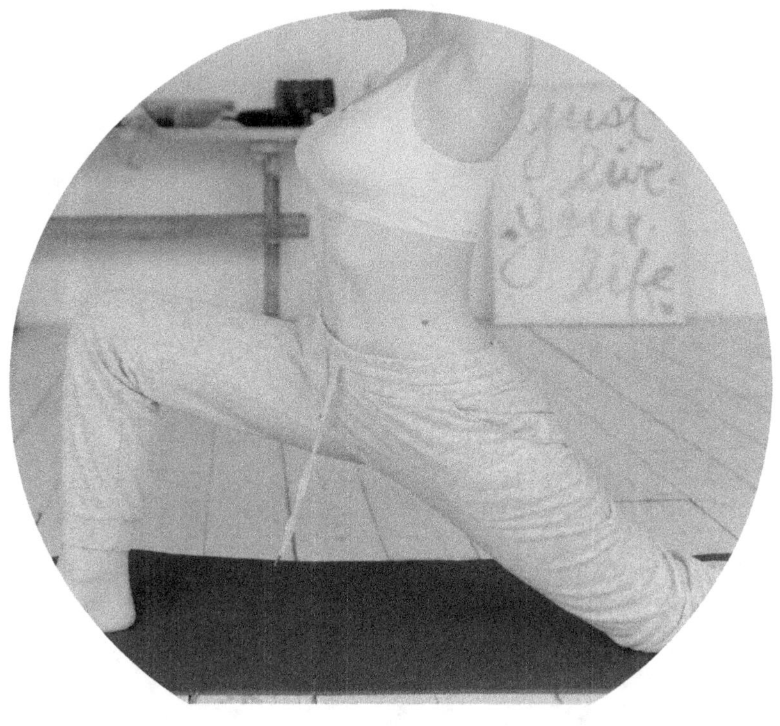

www.ingramcontent.com/pod-product-compliance
Lightning Source LLC
Chambersburg PA
CBHW060909260726
48661CB00008B/3544